COLIN SMITH
'PUTALI BAJE'
(BUTTERFLY GRANDAD)

"Every 'serious' worker, like Colin, who spends years in a region and builds up a picture of the fauna and then writes up his or her findings in an accessible, comprehensive way, and then continues to add further information, corrections and so on, does immeasurable service for our global perspective on butterfly diversity. Many countries, like Nepal, have had few such 'devotees' over the past 100 years or so - which does make Colin's contribution particularly significant."

Dr Richard Irwin Vane-Wright, Associate Member, Durrell Institute of Conservation and Ecology (DICE). University of Kent, UK.

"Colin Smith's work on butterflies of Nepal remains the most exhaustive. He started surveying butterflies in this difficult and demanding terrain when travel and communication were not as easy as they are now. The butterfly-watching community was also small enough that working as a community was nearly impossible. Yet, he did extensive surveys in so many parts of Nepal, meticulously documenting butterflies through the seasons. This generated important information about the occurrence of butterflies in space and time, including their flight periods, which is very important in conservation and ecological studies. I truly admire his perseverance and commitment to the butterfly fauna of the Himalaya. His books will remain a standard reference for a long time."

Dr Krushnamegh Kunte, Associate Professor, National Centre for Biological Sciences (NCBS) Tata Institute of Fundamental Research (TIFR) GKVK Campus, Bellary Road, Bengaluru 560065, India.

COLIN SMITH
'PUTALI BAJE'
(BUTTERFLY GRANDAD)

"One Million footsteps in Nepal"

By
Peter Waine

First published in Great Britain in 2025

Copyright © Peter Waine

The moral right of the author has been asserted.

All rights reserved.

No part of this publication may be reproduced, stored in a retrieval system, or transmitted, in any form or by any means, without the prior permission in writing of the publisher, nor be otherwise circulated in any form of binding or cover other than that in which it is published and without a similar condition including this condition being imposed on the subsequent purchaser.

Front cover photo taken by Nirmal Kumar Thapa, in Pokhara, December 2019.

Cover design by UK Book Publishing and Adam Waine.

Editing, typesetting and publishing by UK Book Publishing.

www.ukbookpublishing.com

ISBN: 978-1-917329-95-8

CONTENTS

Acknowledgements vii

1 Introduction 1

2 Getting Reacquainted 5

3 Early Years in Nepal 11

4 Journey to Nepal, 7,000 miles in 28 days 19

5 Teaching in Nepal 33

6 Butterfly Collections 43

7 Some favourite butterflies 53

8 Butterfly audit of the Annapurna Conservation Area 69

9 Quest for citizenship 83

10 Meeting Colin and seeing Nepal 99

11 A fitting farewell 107

| 12 | Last reflections | 117 |
| 13 | Published works | 123 |

ACKNOWLEDGEMENTS

I want to start by saying a big thank you to everyone who has been a part of this project, whether in a big or small way, from day one. I could not have completed it without your help.

I would never have begun this project had it not been for a chance meeting with Surendra Shrestha at work one day in 2018. Without his energy and support, I may never have reconnected with Colin.

Special thanks go to the wonderful people I met in Nepal in 2022, whose time and hospitality allowed me to visit the places and meet the people mentioned in this book.

I would like to make a special mention of those who were very much part of Colin's life: Min Pariya and his family, who supported Colin for over 30 years, and Surendra Pariya, who learnt all he knows about butterflies from Colin and has taken charge of the Butterfly Museum in Pokhara. I am also deeply grateful to the staff of Green Pastures Hospital - especially Manju, the Palliative Care

Clinical Coordinator, and Dr Ruth Powys, Head of the Palliative Care Unit – for their expertise and kindness in caring for Colin.

To my good friend Jonathan Kemp, one of the first to read this manuscript, thank you for helping me make some necessary changes to improve its flow.

And finally, to my wife Linda – thank you for supporting me when I travelled to Nepal during a difficult time for our family in 2022, and for sitting patiently with me for several days, going through the manuscript and helping me make the changes needed so it all made sense.

I don't read books and I'm not a writer, so this task was a huge undertaking. Many of my friends, knowing that I am dyslexic, asked me who I was going to get to write Colin's biography. But it was a story I was asked to tell, and I felt that I should do whatever was needed to get the job done.

CHAPTER 1

Introduction

My name is Peter Waine. My mother, Muriel Waine, was Muriel Smith before she married. Colin was my mum's cousin, which makes him my second cousin. I would like to be able to say that I knew Colin well and that we were close. The truth is, I didn't know him well, and we didn't keep in touch.

My memories of him are from when I was a young boy of ten years old, living at All Nations College in Ware, Hertfordshire, England. Both my parents were staff at the college, where we had an apartment. Colin was a student, so we saw him quite often. As a child, he appeared massive to me - over six feet tall with very lanky legs. He would tell us he could work out a distance by the number of strides it would take him. He collected butterflies in the college grounds, and a couple of specimens were displayed in our apartment.

I met Colin one more time when he visited my parents during one of his trips to the UK. I remember a comment my mum made after he returned to Nepal. She said he couldn't settle back in England because there was nothing here for him anymore, and that the lifestyle he had adopted in Nepal was too different.

What I didn't realise was the type of life Colin was leading in Nepal, or the contribution he had made to the collection of butterflies. It was only in 2018 (years later) that I became aware of what Colin had been doing. I was working in a private school managing a small team of security guards. When one of my team was absent, we had a security company that provided cover guards.

It was on one of these occasions that a gentleman named Surendra Shrestha came to the school to cover a shift. When I met him, I asked where he was from, and he said Nepal. I mentioned that I had a cousin who lived in Nepal and commented on what a small world it is. Surendra did a couple of Google checks for my cousin, and that's when we discovered that Colin had, in fact, become quite a person of note and was affectionately known as **Putali Baje** (Butterfly Grandad). Surendra told me about an article where Colin had been seeking Nepali citizenship.

Introduction

It was as a result of this new information that I began my research into the present-day Colin Smith. It was clear that although Colin had become well known in Nepal for his butterfly collections, this work was not widely known outside of the country.

With Surendra's help, and through new contacts I made in Nepal, I learned more about Colin and his achievements - building the first collection of butterflies and then writing 24 articles and 13 books (listed at the end of the book).

I also found out that he had written a statement of intent expressing his wish to be treated as a Nepali citizen after

Colin's home Mouse-hole - Photo taken by P Waine 2022

his passing. His desire for citizenship had been strong for many years, and he had submitted multiple applications to the authorities.

With Surendra's support and contacts, I was able to connect with Colin and begin a journey to get to know him again.

In the early days of our conversations, I learned about Colin's deep love for Nepal - its country, and most of all, its people. He was living a simple life that reflected his desire to be like the Nepali people. The love of butterfly collecting that had started as a hobby when he arrived in Nepal in 1966 had turned into a passion to document and celebrate the beautiful diversity of Nepal's butterfly world.

My hope is that when you read this book, you will gain a greater understanding of the butterfly world, the beauty of Nepal, and the wonderful people who embraced Colin as one of their own. It's clear that Colin touched many lives and changed the way people in Nepal appreciate the rich diversity of creatures that inhabit its foothills and mountains.

I hope to explain how Colin's love of God, Nepal, its people, and butterflies made him one of the country's greatest contributors to conservation - and led to him seeking to become a Nepali citizen.

CHAPTER 2

Getting Reacquainted

Having not had any contact with Colin for many years I needed to find a way to speak with him. Surendra contacted his relatives in Pokhara, Nepal, who went to visit Colin. While they were there, they rang Surendra from Colin's phone. Surendra was at work, and he handed me the phone saying, "Colin's on the line." It was an amazing moment. I would use that number many times over the coming months.

It quickly became clear that Colin was quite isolated and living in a fairly remote location near Pokhara. It was also obvious that he had chosen a very simple lifestyle, which he had maintained for many years. I'm convinced this was a matter of choice, not circumstance. He genuinely thought of himself as living a normal Nepali life.

Over the next few months, Surendra and I would talk often - about Colin, about his quest to become a citizen, and about more mundane things like his computer, which had stopped working. Again, Surendra came to the rescue, and some of his family members were able to source and set up a new laptop for Colin.

As my research continued, I discovered that many Nepali people were also trying to help Colin with his quest for Nepali citizenship - a journey he had begun in 1994. It was also clear he was held in high regard. Over 52 years, he had established the two largest and most important collections of butterflies and moths in Nepal.

Surendra told me there was an online campaign to support Colin's application for citizenship. What I didn't expect was that Surendra would take the project on as his own personal mission. He began contacting a wide network of people both in the UK and Nepal.

Suddenly, I wasn't just helping my cousin in his citizenship efforts - I wanted the whole world to know about his achievements.

I felt a growing desire to understand what had motivated Colin to take his place in Nepali history, and why he had fallen in love with the people, the country, and the butterflies of Nepal. I knew I needed to go there, meet the people he had touched, and see the places where he had lived and worked.

After a few conversations with Colin, we began communicating via email - he would check his messages once a week when travelling into Pokhara from his remote home. By this time, it was 2020, and I had planned to visit him in October. Then COVID hit, and all plans were put on hold.

I explained to Colin that I still intended to visit him, and that's when we began talking about writing his biography. He told me that he had once considered writing an autobiography, and in October 2020 he sent me this email:

Dear Peter,

I can write to you better now from my home computer and copy it when I get to the office. You should by now have all six parts of my autobiography. Personally, I find it very boring! I can put down the facts, but I cannot generally make good stories out of them. The one thing I haven't written was what I had planned to name it - "One Million Footsteps in Nepal".

This book was to be based on the weekly letters I wrote to my mother, which are now with Arnold, my older brother.

If he can get them (or copies of them) to you, then you could write it for me! This would be a great help.

All for now, God bless, **Colin**

Receiving that email made me even more determined to follow through. His story - far from boring - deserved to be told and celebrated. His contribution to conservation and the natural history of Nepal needed to be more widely recognised.

I contacted Colin's brother Arnold, who lives in New Zealand with his daughter and her family on a farm in Cambridge, Waikato.

Although I'd known Arnold and Kate before, we hadn't been in touch for at least 30 years. Colin and Arnold had not seen each other in many years and only had occasional phone calls or emails, mostly because of Colin's remote location.

I communicated mainly with Kate by email to check in on Arnold and whether they were still in contact with Colin, as his computer was broken. Over the following months, I was able to rekindle a friendship with the family and joined in on several Zoom meetings they had with Colin - some of which happened while I was in Nepal in 2022.

That connection became another unexpected gift from this whole journey.

I was thrilled when Arnold told me he still had a lot of Colin's paperwork, including the letters Colin had sent to his parents between 1966 and 1987. He also had a large number of newsletters Colin had written during his mission contract. Arnold sent them to me, and they became a rich source of background information about Colin's lifestyle, thoughts, and concerns during those years - things you'd only share with your family when you're far away.

I had no idea that a chance meeting with Surendra Shrestha would lead me on this path - reconnecting with Colin in Nepal, renewing ties with Arnold and Kate, and getting to know her husband Grant and their boys, Sam and James, in New Zealand.

I'll return to Colin's quest for citizenship later in the book, but first, I want to introduce you to Colin's early journey in Nepal.

CHAPTER 3

Early Years Before Nepal

Colin Philip Smith was born on 24th November 1936 in North London, in Highgate N6, where he lived with his older brother Arnold and their parents, Ebenezer and Rose Smith. He started his schooling at Highgate Primary School and later attended Tollington High School, a grammar school, where he was awarded a state scholarship to study at Imperial College, South Kensington, London, in the summer of 1955.

Colin states in his memoirs that he felt it was a privilege to have been brought up in a Christian family. One of his earliest memories, at around six years old, was being worried at bedtime. He asked his mother, "What would happen to me if I died in the night?" (They were living in London at the time, which was being bombed nightly by the

Germans, so the question was a serious one.) His mother replied that he would go straight to be with Jesus, and that satisfied him. The family were regular churchgoers and were members of a local Baptist church.

While at Highgate Primary School, he became fascinated by maths, which he later studied at university, continuing on to complete a second degree in Number Theory at University College.

During this time in Highgate, he visited his maternal aunt, Joyce, in Kingsbury. Her husband, Bob, had collected butterflies in his youth and had a marvellous collection housed in a 12-drawer cabinet.

In 1950, Colin joined the Boy Scouts (18th Finchley Troop), and that summer attended a camp at Cranham Woods in Gloucestershire. He was so impressed with the butterflies there that he became determined to start collecting them himself. With Uncle Bob's help, he began collecting during a family holiday in Clevedon, Somerset, where he caught a **Small Blue** - the smallest British butterfly.

From then on, he collected butterflies on other holidays and locally on Hampstead Heath, where he caught **Chimney Sweeper** moths. In Hadley Woods, he caught four **White Admirals**, and in Epping Forest, four **Purple Hairstreaks** high in the oak trees of Pear Tree Plain - very difficult to catch. In Hockridge Wood near Berkhamsted, he found **Orange Underwings** (also moths, high on silver birch trees), and **Marbled Whites** in a field beside Whippendell Woods, Watford. Uncle Bob also took him to Princes Risborough, where they caught a **Green Hairstreak** - very hard to spot among the green leaves. It was there he also caught his first and only **Duke of Burgundy Fritillary**.

Memories from his brother, Dr Arnold Smith (now living in New Zealand):

I have few memories of Colin's earliest years. The five-and-a-half-year age gap didn't lend itself to us being playmates. But around the start of the war (circa 1939-40), our cousin Thelma lived with us at Priory Gardens, London, and later in Potter Street, and the three of us children did quite a lot together.

In 1940, we moved to Bournemouth. With the war, Dad was seconded from the Land Registry to the Home Office, Aliens Department. He told us he worked on applications for release from internment - mostly from Italian ice cream sellers. At the end of 1940, the department was moved out of London to Bournemouth 'for the duration of the war', so we moved too.

It always struck me as ironic. We stayed in London through most of the Blitz, only to move south in time for the 'tip-and-run' raids on coastal towns. Then they moved us back again just in time for the V1 and V2 German rockets!

*While in Bournemouth, we were visited by Aunty Joyce (Mum's youngest sister) and her fiancé Arnold Turner, who became Uncle Bob. He was an engineer, had a car, and was a keen 'bug-hunter' - a butterfly collector. Colin and I were fascinated by it, which later became a passion for me and a career for Colin. They had a successful collecting trip along the coast. Bob gave me a net and Coleman's book on English butterflies - both of which I still have. That summer, I began collecting (mostly **Cabbage Whites**), but Colin's enthusiasm would flourish later.*

In 1960, Dad retired, and we moved to Chesham in the Chilterns. I'd passed my driving test and bought my first car (a Morris 10). Of course, we explored for butterflies. I remember a piece of woodland with many sallow trees ('pussy willow'), whose fluffy flowers attracted insects. We'd go at night, spread a sheet under the branches and tap the trees with a stick. The insects would fall, too drunk on nectar to fly, and we'd pick out the ones we wanted.

One spring, Dad came with us, and I parked the car on a woodland ride. After our successful hunt, we returned to find the car doors open, two police cars, and several officers. Apparently, there had been local arson trouble, and neighbours had reported our group 'with torches'. The woods straddled a county boundary, so two constabularies had responded. They even had more police waiting at the other end of the wood! They thought they'd caught poachers or vandals - until they saw our butterfly haul. The situation ended in laughter, and they asked us to notify them next time we planned a nocturnal expedition!

*Years later, around 1983, I was living in Sheffield when a colleague offered me 'some old insect boxes' from a neighbour's house clearance. I wasn't hopeful, but it turned out to be 56 Edwardian biscuit tins packed with papered butterflies from John Hewett, a late museum curator. He'd worked in Sarawak and later South Africa. Before his death, he reviewed the specimens and dismissed them as worthless, but I saved them from being destroyed. Colin happened to be in England at the time, working with Paul Smart (author of Butterflies of the World). He took some of the specimens to be identified - some turned out to be quite valuable, including an **Atlas moth**, a **Rajah Brooke's Birdwing**, and two specimens that went to the Natural History Museum: one, the first known male of a rare species; the other, a new subspecies.*

After finishing university, Colin became a schoolteacher, though he found it wasn't for him. He looked into lecturing and was offered a post at Glasgow University. He enjoyed teaching maths, but lecturers were expected to publish research. After three years as Assistant Lecturer with no research published, he told his professor (Rankin) that he believed the teaching was more important. The professor offered him a fourth and final year, after which Colin prepared for missionary work. (Interestingly, Colin's father had once hoped to go to India as a missionary but couldn't because of family responsibilities. He supported Colin fully.)

Colin joined All Nations Missionary College in 1963, partly because it was in Buckinghamshire, near home. He had been away from home for most of the past four years and expected to leave again after the two-year course. During this time, he also helped at Hivings Park Sunday School, where he created dramatised Bible stories for children, using makeshift props. He even considered writing a "Dramatised Bible" but never got beyond a few scenes.

Another reason for choosing All Nations was the Bursar, Rev. Ron Waine - his cousin's husband - they had been missionaries in Algeria. Colin found the courses quite challenging, but also deeply interesting, especially Philosophy of Religion and Rev. Pawson's New Testament classes.

The college later moved to Easneye, near Ware in Hertfordshire, to a house with deep Christian connections to the Buxton family. (Sir Thomas Buxton had championed the Emancipation of Slaves Bill in 1832, and his wife Hannah had hoped the mansion would be used by faithful servants of God.)

At Easneye, Colin was encouraged to take up a hobby for the mission field. When he mentioned his love of butterflies, they asked him to create a local collection, which he did, even donating his best cabinet to house it.

His interest in mission work centred on the Indian subcontinent, so in his final year he contacted all mission societies working in that region. He explained that he had been a university teacher and asked if there were any opportunities. A few replied saying there were none at the time, but the **Regions Beyond Missionary Union** phoned the college and invited him to London to meet their Executive Director, Mr Ernest Oliver.

Mr Oliver was about to leave on a tour of the region, and, after interviewing Colin, promised to look into options. Upon his return, he offered Colin two posts: one at a large boys' school in India, the other with United Mission to Nepal, teaching at a mission school in Luitel in the Gorkha hills.

To cut a long story short - **Nepal won**. (Oliver had previously worked there himself.)

Colin already knew quite a bit about Nepal from helping at Himalayan Helper Camps for kids run by Mrs Peta Craven at Cloverley Hall, Whitchurch UK, with the International Nepal Fellowship.

CHAPTER 4

Journey to Nepal, 7,000 Miles in 28 Days

A few friends gathered at Chesham Station at 8am on the morning of 13th January 1966 to see Colin off. Colin, along with his parents and brother, boarded the train to London and then continued on to Liverpool. Due to labour troubles at the docks, Colin had to detour via Birkenhead. There was a short amount of time for the family to explore the ship and have tea in the lounge before all visitors were requested to leave by 4:30pm.

Colin Smith 'Putali Baje' (Butterfly Grandad)

RMS Circassia (III) departing for her final voyage
to India on 13th January 1966

C Deck Dining Room *Sports/Sun Deck*

Promenade Deck (lounges, lobby, gallery, reading/
writing rooms, library)

Main Lounge   The Long Gallery

(All interior and deck photos sourced from a 1960s brochure via www.ssmaritime.com by Dr Reuben Goossens, Maritime Historian)

The following are excerpts from Colin's journal, recording his journey:

After you left, I unpacked and sorted myself out. Then came dinner - five courses (more if you wanted them). There was an infinite variety - the only difficulty was deciphering the menu. (I wish they'd write it in English instead of French.)

Saturday 15th - It's calmer now than earlier today when things were sliding all over the dressing table. We must be nearly across the Bay of Biscay, though there's still no land in sight. They keep putting the clocks forward, but as we're still going west, this means we're getting out of sync with the sun.

Sunday 16th - The sea is like a millpond. Still can't see much of Spain though. There was a church service this morning at 10:30. My stomach is settled now and my appetite's returning.

Monday 17th - The Rock of Gibraltar was a most impressive sight... it's now slipped back into the sea. Life aboard has become very pleasant - and rather lazy.

Letter from - Gibraltar

Colin devoted much of his letter to the food on board, not being used to the opulence of cruise-liner cuisine.

> *"There's an infinite variety - the only difficulty is deciphering the menu. For breakfast, there are ten cereals, 15 egg dishes and 19 kinds of jam and marmalade. You can have as much as you want. This morning, I counted 19 dishes without eggs - that means 34 different main courses for breakfast!"*

He also noted the opportunity to play chess and table tennis (although the latter was cancelled due to wind blowing the balls away).

Wednesday 19th - Keep finding more missionaries on board - we're planning to have a Bible study.

Thursday 20th - Just returned from a short visit ashore in Malta. The place looks like London after the war - derelict and drab. The harbour is extensive, and some cute little tugs pushed us in. We had 24 people at our first Bible study this evening. Philippians 1:1-8 - good discussion. Lots of interesting people on board. I usually have a decent talk with someone new each day.

Letter from - Malta

Colin commented on the change in weather and how it brought everyone out onto the sun deck:

> *"It's like June in England - when the sun shines. Life is very pleasant and lazy; a holiday atmosphere prevails."*

He added:

> *"I've been having one or two Indian curries - just to start getting used to them. I quite like them, but they're hot! Not like your curry - more like bhaji."*

Sunday 23rd - At Port Said for about two hours. It was very impressive to wake up this morning and see 50 ships queuing to enter the Suez. I really feel like I'm in the East now - little boats crowd around to sell their wares. Lovely leatherwork. A magician came aboard - 'Gulli-Gulli' - and performed tricks, producing chickens out of the most unlikely places. We've now entered the Red Sea. Just passed Sinai. Most exciting, but too far off to photograph. Beautiful sunset.

Letter from – Port Said

Colin described the spectacle of the Suez Canal, the crew switching to white uniforms, and his first swim in the on-board pool:

> *"Most cool and refreshing - because it's really hot. A beautiful sunset, with the thinnest crescent moon."*

> *"We saw flying fish - tiny, like dragonflies - and porpoises rubbing against the ship to scrape off barnacles."*

Tuesday 25th - It's now hotter than it ever gets in England. The crew have switched to white shorts. There's air conditioning in the dining room, which makes it feel like going from a fridge into a Turkish bath. I'm eating well trying to work out how to use all five knives, forks, and spoons they give us. I managed with only one spoon and two forks today - my best effort yet.

Friday 28th - Just returned to the ship from Aden. Fascinating contrast - whitewashed European-style homes beside patchwork shacks of wood and tin. Not that the locals are poor - they just live that way. Armed troops with machine guns are everywhere, but life goes on.

Letter from - Aden

"We didn't leave until the middle of the night, but the little boats did a brisk trade. Someone bought a typewriter like mine for £18. Kodachrome film was 24 shillings instead of 36. They had toy dogs that walked, sat, wagged tails, and yapped battery operated.

I wasn't going to buy anything, but outward-bound prices are better (no British Customs). I bought 7x50 prismatic binoculars for £5 - case and strap included. Mr McPherson bought an Agfa Silette camera (better than mine) for £10 - worth at least £25."

Sunday 30th - Not much to report. We stopped mid-afternoon - engine trouble.

Monday 31st - Weather's constantly warm. I spend most of my time on the sun deck reading, writing, talking, or sleeping. We keep putting the clocks forward. By tomorrow we'll be five hours ahead of you. Dreamily chugging through the vast Arabian Sea. We'll reach Bombay on Wednesday but can't go ashore till Thursday. It's been a good trip - I've read a lot and made many friends. England feels very far away now.

Thursday 3rd Feb - Bombay - We've arrived. The travel agent didn't know I was coming, so no train seat was booked across India. He said the trains were fully booked for two days - but there might be cancellations. He arranged for my luggage (four boxes, two trunks, two suitcases, one briefcase, one holdall, and a tent!) to go to the station. After a few calls and about an hour's wait, a seat became available on the 9:45pm train.

Letter from - Bombay

"From the ship, Bombay looked Western. But walking its streets, it's clearly Indian - the smells, the rich and the poor.

Everyone's trying to cheat you. I thought the East would be spiritual (not necessarily Christian), but I find it just as materialistic as England."

Friday 4th - I'm on the train, in a sort of four-berth sleeper - only three of us, so plenty of room. Everyone speaks English, sort of. This express train travels at 20mph - I wonder what the slow ones are like!

Saturday 5th - In the Lucknow waiting room. The train journey hasn't been too bad. We were two hours late (36 hours in all). The train stops every mile or two. I have a three-hour wait for my next train. The land started flat and dry, now it's greener. Funny - endless countryside, then a station in the middle of nowhere. Now on the Kanpur Express to Muzaffarpur. Bought food: 8 bananas and 4 oranges for 1 rupee. Cattle wander through stations. No one bats an eye. One man carrying a suitcase on his head overtook our train. Coolies carry multiple cases on their heads - charging 8 or 9 rupees.

Sunday 6th - Still on a train. This one's even slower and bumpier. I nearly missed my change at Muzaffarpur in the early hours - only woke up because one of my companions nudged me. Made it just in time to jump on the adjoining train. This is the last one. Countryside is greener now. Stations are swarming with hawkers chanting their wares.

Worst part of train travel? Dust. It gets into everything. Saw some exotic birds and butterflies from the window.

Raxaul - At last! Dr Trevor Strong from Duncan Hospital met me at the station. I'm staying in the bungalow with him, his wife, and their three children. They're home on holidays, and I'm helping Joan with maths and physics. The hospital is lovely. Quite a few patients attend optional church services. We're right on the Indian border - only 200 yards across the river is Nepal.

Had my first official Nepali language lesson. For lunch, a mild curry. English-style meal in the evening. They grow English vegetables here.

Thursday 10th - Up at 5am to catch the 6:30am bus. Delayed by passport and customs, so we actually boarded at 7am. Didn't leave till 8am. The sign said Kathmandu was 128 miles - seems odd as it's only 42 miles by plane.

The first 20 miles were flat - partly jungle, partly farmland. Then we climbed. And climbed. Hairpin bend after hairpin bend. Steep rocky gorges, dry riverbeds, terraced slopes. We reached 8,000 feet before descending into a valley - cultivated even on 45-degree slopes.

I was fine, still used to the ship. But I think my companion Dr Bill Gould was feeling sick with all the bumping and swaying. We reached Kathmandu at 6pm - an average speed of 12.8mph over ten hours. We caught up with and overtook three other buses that had left before us.

The mountains were partly hidden by clouds - just one glimpse of snow-capped peaks.

Colin's journey to Nepal 1966 - Map created by Adam Waine 2025

Train = orange **Boat = yellow** **Bus = red**

1. London to Liverpool.
2. Liverpool board the RMS Circassia (III) to Bombay.
3. Gibraltar.
4. Malta.
5. Port Said (Egypt).
6. Aden (now Yemen).
7. Bombay (now Mumbai) to Lucknow.
8. Lucknow.
9. Muzaffarpur.
10. Raxaul to Kathmandu.
11. Kathmandu.

I'm staying with an American family until Bill goes to Tansen next week - then I'll move into the mission HQ.

Kathmandu - Friday 11th - Went shopping with the ladies this morning to get my bearings. It's a fantastic place with an old-world charm. The fruit market is lovely - anything you want at decent prices. Other shops are unlike anywhere else but sell everything.

Carvings and shrines are everywhere. Truly, Kathmandu has more temples than houses - and more gods than people.

First impressions of Nepal
(from Colin's journal)

These 200 square miles have seen more fortunes made and empires fall than Paris or Sudan. Their record of political assassinations makes the Tower of London look like a hospital! The fertile soil supports 500,000 people. The same mud makes bricks for their homes, but no one minds that the rice fields sink lower each year.

Homes - two storeys, thatched or tiled roofs - blend beautifully with the landscape of bamboo, gum trees, bottlebrush, and terraced fields. Nepal's ingenious irrigation and hillside farming impresses from the outset.

Kathmandu – the road to Paradise. You feel sympathy for St Paul on Mars Hill. People here blend Animism with Hinduism and Buddhism. It's the Newar carvings that give Nepali buildings such charm – but many temples still bear scars from the 1934 earthquake, and some are near collapse.

Sadly, modern cement-rendered pillbox houses offer no architectural replacement. The Nepali are great at starting things – they love an opening ceremony – but maintenance isn't as much of a focus. Perhaps it's religious: building earns merit, but repairs don't. That may explain the crumbling temples.

The people are friendly. On the roads, drivers pull over to let you pass – otherwise you'd be stuck forever. Villages are full of bright-eyed children smiling from all directions. Everyone says 'Namaste'. They don't pester or pander. They treat you as an equal – sometimes slightly less so, due to caste. The youth are eager for education, keen to engage with the modern world. The older generation remains traditional.

CHAPTER 5

Teaching in Nepal

Colin went to Nepal to teach. He was picked to teach in a school in Luitel; however, this was changed while in Kathmandu and he was requested to go to Pokhara on 1st June. The reason for this change was due to people in Pokhara requesting the Mission to start a new (private) boarding school there. (At present, there were only government schools, or else a seven-day walk to Kathmandu.) So, together with an experienced missionary from International Nepal Fellowship, Miss Pat Mabey, a Nepali headmistress from Gorkha, Mrs Martha Mukhiya, and one other Nepali teacher, Mr Bhojraj Marahatta, Colin was co-opted as teacher, business manager and treasurer of the School Board.

Colin describes his first impressions:

> *Pokhara was (and still is) delightful and my favourite place in Nepal. (It was much smaller in those days – 10 or 15 thousand people, as against its present 150,000.) It also has the best view of mountains anywhere in Nepal. The clear views of the complete Annapurna range of 8,000m peaks, viewed from just 800 metres altitude and only 60km away. They are dominated by Machha Puchare, 6,900m, but only 30km away. It is a bottle-shaped valley with Pokhara city in the neck of the bottle, down the centre of which runs the Seti River. It is also famous for its three lakes: Rara, Tilicho and Shey-Poksundo, fed by the local streams, not the Himalayan snows.*

The new school had been in preparation since 1965, when the local people wanted to bring in quality education. "We want our boys in a good boarding school where there will be disciplined living." They decided on a name for the school: 'Nepali Ideal School', although when the school was opened it was given the name Nepali Adarsh Vidyalaya. The Managing Board was set up in late 1965 and then spent the next nine months in discussions, inspection of possible sites, and dealing with finance and staff.

The official opening of the school was on 11th June 1966. There were three temporary bamboo and thatched buildings for a dormitory, classrooms, and a staff house. The kitchen and dining room were just bamboo. The construction was very temporary, and on one occasion the roof was blown away. All the buildings were in a two-acre field in Battuel Chaw village. By October 1966 there were five teachers including Colin and a hostel warden. The boarders were very eager and would spend some of their lunchtime just waiting in their seats for lessons to begin. The boarders enjoyed games, especially football (which was played in bare feet). They also enjoyed simple board games and experimenting with a magnifying glass.

At the school, they started with just four classes, with plans to add one each year. There were 60 boys, some of whom had previously been in higher classes in government schools. The boys were a delight to teach - eager to learn, and tolerant of Colin's broken Nepali. Pokhara had no electricity at that time, and they used paraffin lamps (also a paraffin refrigerator) and candles. Colin found some ink pots that had been fitted with a wick and glass on top, and half a dozen of them placed around the room gave very good general light.

Picture from booklet about the school 1967 (Fly a Kite)

When Colin started, he was living at the end of the boys' hostel and eating with them, but later moved out to hire two rooms in Battuel Chaw village (for 50 rupees per month – the equivalent of 29 pence in today's money) and had a local boy cook meals for him. He couldn't have toast for breakfast since there was no bread available in Pokhara then. There were plenty of eggs, so he made do with scotch pancakes instead. Later, he built his own house on the school field out of bamboo and thatch for just 750 rupees (£4.35) and lived in it for 18 months. While there, he had one of the schoolboys cook for him, in return for which he helped with his fees.

Colin eventually rented a house in the village of Battuel Chaw with mosquito wire windows and a corrugated iron roof. He was the only Westerner in the village. He lived on a diet of porridge (from Kathmandu), eggs (local), soup (from England), potatoes (local, but like marbles), and meat and vegetables (once in a blue moon). Also fruit (bananas and pineapples), custard, margarine (from Hong Kong), and home-made bread rolls, buns and jam. Colin had about ten classes a week and did the school accounts.

Saturdays at the boarding school were occupied in the mornings with cleaning out the boys' hostel - taking all the beds out and thoroughly cleaning the (mud) floor, while the boys would wash their clothes. Then, in the afternoons, the staff would take them for walks. There were just three teachers, so the students were divided into juniors and seniors, and one of the staff would stay on duty at the school. Colin would often take the seniors and less frequently the juniors. The walks were like *Alice in the Looking Glass* in that, whatever way they started, they nearly always ended up at a river - where they would plunge in.

One day, when it was Colin's turn for duty at the school, he had an encounter with a cow which wandered into the school premises. The boundary wall was just loose stones piled up and easily broken down by cattle. When cows encroached on the school grounds, the boys would throw stones to drive them out - especially now, as the boys had been making themselves gardens.

On this occasion, the cow got in while he was on duty with no one else there. Colin took a stone and threw it near the cow. Unfortunately, it ran right into the path of the stone, which bounced off the ground and hit it on the back of the neck. Its front legs were paralysed! When the boys returned, they fed it grass and dragged it outside the gate (so it wouldn't die on their compound). It could not survive and died a day or so later.

Under the law of Nepal, it was the death penalty if you killed a cow! This left Colin with a serious issue. The village elders called a meeting. First, they said it was a bull, not a cow - so there was no question of the death penalty. The only question was how to recompense the owner. He demanded Rs.400 (the equivalent of £20 in UK money), but the others disagreed. No - it wasn't worth that much; it was an old one. In the end, they fixed the price at Rs.100. Then the village chief said:

> *"Look, this foreigner has come here to help us, so to show there is no ill-feeling against him, I'll pay the first Rs.10 myself, and he can just pay Rs.90."*

After teaching for two years at the Pokhara boys' school, Colin went on to teach maths at the school in Luitel, which is where he was originally going to start his time in Nepal. While teaching at this school, Colin set up a voluntary 'Science Club' for some of the students.

Some of them were keen to look through his telescope at the craters of the moon, the four planets of Jupiter, or the rings of Saturn. One of his students was Upendra Devkota, who became a neurosurgeon and was the founder of the first neurological trauma unit in Nepal. Another of Colin's students was Baburam Bhattarai, who went on to be a politician and served as Prime Minister between 2011 and 2013. Colin only spent a year at the school, and then returned to Pokhara, where he took up a post as physics teacher on the Prithivi Narayan College Campus.

In 1971, Colin returned to the boarding school for one more year. He would be teaching the same students he had taught in class five years earlier. The school had four houses: Dhaulagiri, Annapurna, Machapuchare and Lamjung. All students were placed in one of the houses, with about 33 or 34 students in each. There was a staff supervisor, and the students of each house were responsible for electing a house leader and deputy. The houses had various activities through which they could earn points, and the house with the most points at the end of the year would win the Cup of Honour.

House activities and marks could be earned from classroom work, general knowledge quizzes, spelling contests, and personal interest projects. Points could also be earned for games and track-and-field sports. Winning was dependent on teamwork and the effort of all the house members.

During Colin's final year, the school produced a new prospectus which received approval from the District Education Committee. It stated that the school would be open as a high school, with extra classes in years eight, nine and ten. Classes would have a minimum of 25 students, include vocational classes, and be primarily a boarding school. The school had around 160 students, which filled all the hostel accommodation. Ongoing building work continued with a crew of 65 men, working mainly on two new buildings for the school. Discussions at district level were being held about the need for extra land, and improvements to the water supply and electricity.

Colin's last year of teaching in 1971 would mark the end of his time in education in Nepal, and the beginning of full and part-time work catching and cataloguing butterflies for the Natural History Museum of Nepal and the Butterfly

Museum in Pokhara. It also marked the end of support from the mission society in the UK, which had been responsible for sending Colin to Nepal.

CHAPTER 6

Butterfly Collections

In 1963, Dorothy Mierow travelled to Nepal as a Peace Corps volunteer to teach Geography at the new Prithwi Narayan Campus, which was led by a man from India, George John. In 1965, the construction of the museum began on an isolated patch of land on the outskirts of the P.N. campus.

Photo from book '30 Years in Pokhara' by Dorothy Mierow

Colin Smith 'Putali Baje' (Butterfly Grandad)

Dorothy describes in her book *30 Years in Pokhara* how she meets up with Colin and invites him to set up a butterfly display in the museum:

> *The Porch of the Maidens of ancient Greece inspired me to have carved figures of five different ethnic groups of Nepal placed to support the roof of the porch in front of the museum. In this way, the museum would get a colourful appearance, and villagers who walked a long way to see the museum would see something even if the museum was closed.*

Photo of Butterfly Museum entrance by P. Waine, 2022

These ten figures were carved in Cottage Industries in Kathmandu and represented people that live in different regions of Nepal: Tibetans from the mountains, Gurungs from the hills, Tharus of the lowland plains, and the Brahmins and Newars of Kathmandu.

Shortly after the museum was built, Colin Smith came from England to teach at the newly established Gandaki Boarding School. He collected and knew a lot about butterflies. I asked him to collect butterflies for the museum, and Mr John assured him that if he were to design cases and cabinets for the butterflies he collected, the college would pay to have them built for the museum.

Colin stayed on and taught mathematics at the campus and enlarged his butterfly collection. He has been with the museum in Pokhara from its start and has built up a collection of equal size for the university at their museum in Swayambunath, Kathmandu. The insects, especially the moths and butterflies, are well kept and have attracted so much attention that the museum used to be called 'The Butterfly Museum'."

(Taken from the book "Thirty Years in Pokhara" by Dorothy Mierow)

Butterfly cabinets at the Butterfly Museum, Pokhara - Photo taken by P. Waine, 2022

The museum is now looked after by Mr Surendra Pariya, who is employed by the Annapurna National Park. Surendra was a young man when he met Colin and travelled with him on a number of occasions when he was collecting specimens. Surendra also learnt the art of displaying and cataloguing the specimens.

Over the years, Surendra has become an expert in this field and has given talks regarding the collection and the wider field of butterflies. The museum still stands where it was built in 1965, and the collections of the various groups of butterflies and moths are still in the original cabinets, which Surendra cares for as part of his duties. I had the pleasure of meeting Surendra when I travelled out to Nepal in October 2022. He was my personal guide during my stay and introduced me to a number of people who had been part of Colin's life in Nepal.

Butterfly collectors from all over the world have travelled to Nepal and taken their specimens back to museums in the UK, Europe and Japan. Unfortunately, this practice continues to this day. However, the move away from specimen collection to digital photography has halted the mass exodus of some of the rare and endemic species.

Colin before his digital photo days (from Colin's photo album)

The history of butterflying in Nepal dates back to General Thomson Hardwick, who started studying them in Nepal in 1826. Maj. W.G.H. Gough (1835) attempted to collate a list of butterfly species in Nepal for the first time by recording 150 species. Then after, Major General Ramsey accounted for 44 species during 1852-67. Lt. Colonel F.M. Bailey (1951) issued a list of 365 species. In 1970, a Japanese expedition to Kathmandu and East Nepal came up with a list of 285 species, out of which eight or ten species or subspecies were new to science.

In the Butterfly Museum at Pokhara, there are 857 butterfly species, of which 694 are from Nepal. Similarly, 750 moth species are in the collection. Besides these, the museum has 67 species in a *Colias* collection from the Eurasian region, and 60 species of *Parnassius* from the same area. There are 104 species in an Oriental collection, which includes *Amathusiid*, Oak-leaves, Swordtails and *Euthalia* butterflies. Finally, there are 172 species from different parts of the world. When Colin started to collect butterflies, there was a list of 365, and now in the museum, there are 694 different species – so you can see that the number has nearly doubled in that time.

There has been a steady stream of visitors to the museum over the years, with the average number in the early

2,000s being up to 18,000 visitors a year. That has reduced in recent times to about 9,000. There is a steady stream of Nepalese students and quite a few from overseas who visit for their studies of butterflies.

It was while Colin was teaching in Swayambhu that Dr Uprety (Professor of Zoology at Tribhuvan University) called him to his office in Kirtipur and suggested that he collect butterflies of Nepal for them to help form the first Natural History Museum in Kathmandu, which opened in 1975. Colin collected between 1974 and 1978 to establish an Entomology section. This was Colin's first contract to collect butterflies, which enabled him to visit some of the furthest districts of Nepal. He records that on one journey he went to the far west of Nepal, which he had not visited previously.

Natural History Museum in Kathmandu -
Photo taken by P. Waine, 2022

To date, there are more than 13,000 butterfly specimens, of which Colin's contribution is approximately 70%. Some of the specimens are on display; however, most are in cabinets that are locked away in a side room. I was able to view them - these can be viewed by visitors on request. I visited in October 2022.

I'm sure Colin never imagined when he travelled to Nepal in 1966 that he would be responsible for setting up the two main collections of Nepalese butterflies and moths in Nepal .

The following are the main collections of Butterflies and Moths that Colin has been responsible for.

- **Natural History Museum, Swayambhu** - *Butterflies of Nepal by region to show variations across the country - e.g. agestor from Central Nepal and agestor govindra from West Nepal, Dragon Fly Collection (checked by Mr Graham Vick)*

- **Kathmandu University Collection, Dhulikhel** - *Butterflies and Moths of Nepal (Most complete collection of Moths in Nepal)*

- **Annapurna Regional Museum, P.N. Campus** - *Butterflies, Moths & Dragonflies of Nepal*

- **Specimens from other countries** – *The major other collection was the **snow apollo** one. Dorothy Mierow had once worked for Avinoff, who interested her in these butterflies and who suggested "we make a collection of them at Pokhara. Now our most expensive butterfly was female of **Parnassius autocraor** that had been described by Avinoff and cost me 99p". (Colin's words)*

- *World-wide collection representing sub-families plus collections of **clouded yellows**, **Oakleaves**, **Anathsiidae**, **Swordtails**, and Comparisons between Europe, Nepal & Japan.*

CHAPTER 7

Some favourite butterflies

I couldn't write about Colin without having some pictures of butterflies. You can see from the list at the rear of this book that he has written 13 books, and published many articles so I don't intend to replicate those.

I asked a few of Colin's butterfly colleagues if they could send me a list of some of Colin's favourite butterflies. Between them they sent me a list of 26 species which I have reduced to the 16 I have photographs of.

Piet Van Der Poel (**PVDP**)
Mahendra Singh Limbu (**MSL**)
Surendra Pariyar (**SP**)

These photographs were taken by Piet Van Der Poel and Mahendra Singh Limbu except the Nepal Wall, which is very rare.

A Papilionoidea – Swallowtails

1 Krishna Peacock, *Papilio krishna* Moore, 1858

In 1994, Colin proposed Krishna's Peacock to be adopted as Nepal's National Butterfly. It is a striking, big butterfly that one immediately recognizes as not being any of the other Peacocks. And it being named after Krishna, the Hindu god of protection, compassion and love, gives it a special significance for Nepalese. Thirty years down the road there is still not a national butterfly. ***(PVDP)***

Krishna Peacock, from Bhutan

2 Common Red Apollo, *Parnassius epaphus* Oberthür, 1879

Apollos are high altitude specialists and Colin tried to collect Apollo species from the Himalayas and beyond in the Natural History Museum in Pokhara. Each valley in Nepal has its own subspecies. In 1983, he even described a subspecies, *P. epaphus chiddi*, from Mugu. Unfortunately, this subspecies was later synonymized with *P. epaphus capdevillei*. **(PVDP)**

Common Red Apollo, Manang

3 Kaiser-i-Hind *Teinopalpus imperialis* Hope, 1843

This rare, bright green, ochre and yellow species flies mostly among the treetops, but may come down to earth later in the morning. On one trip in Godavari, Colin was trying to collect some specimens, but they were up in the trees, and it started to rain. He sat down and waited for the sun to come back, which happened an hour later and then one Kaiser-i-Hind crawled out of the grass right in front of him, having been hiding in full view. It is worth waiting for. *(PVDP)*

This is certainly very interesting as it is not known to feed on flowers and come to any nutrients in its adult life span. **(MSL)**

Kaiser-I-Hind, from Bhutan ©: Karma Wangdi

Its rich green and purple colouration has made this one of the magnificent butterflies. Flies between 7000-8000 ft on hill tops for a short period in very few numbers, active in early morning. All this character has made it prized by most of the collectors across the world. **(SP)**

4 Golden Birdwing, *Troides aeacus* Felder & Felder, 1860

These are spectacular butterflies and with a wingspan measuring nearly six inches, are the largest species flying in Nepal. These are also protected worldwide. **(MSL)**

Fairly common throughout Nepal, it is recorded from 1,100 - 6,000 ft in March to July. The adults can be found feeding on thistles in West Nepal. **(CS Butterflies of Nepal, No 42)**

Golden Birdwing Nepal Smith

B Hesperiidae family – skippers

5 Striped Dawnfly, *Capila jayadeva* Moore, 1866

The three dawnflies that Colin collected in Nepal in the late 1980s and early 1990s all came from a small wet subtropical rainforest area below Num in Sankhuwasabha, in east Nepal. The area was later bulldozed to make room for a hydroelectric project. None of these dawnflies had ever been seen anywhere else in Nepal. But then, on 4 November 2012, when Colin was doing an inventory of the butterfly species that visited the yellow Poinsettia near his house in Pokhara, one showed up to say "hello". *(PVDP)*

Striped Dawnfly, from Bhutan © Kado Rinchen

C Pieridae – Whites (and Yellows) family

6 Sherpa White, now: Chumbi White, *Sinopieris chumbiensis sherpae* Epstein, 1979

Colin paid special attention to species that had been described from Nepal, which started in 1826 with the Rose Windmill swallowtail. The Sherpa White was described as *Pontia sherpae* by Colin's friend Hans Epstein in 1979. Recently, it has been placed as a subspecies of *Sinopieris chumbiensis* (de Nicéville, 1897). In Nepal, it was only known from the Annapurna area, but recently it has also been found in the Karnali area. *(PVDP)*

Chumbi White, Manang

D Lycaenidae family – hairstreaks, blues and coppers

7 Broad Spark, *Sinthusa chandrana* Moore, 1882

In his 2011 guidebook to the butterflies of the Annapurna area, Colin described the Broad Spark as a "delightful" species. In his pictorial guidebook of 2015, Colin wrote: "Its flight is very fast, so that the brilliant blue of the upper side does give the impression of a flying delightful little spark. It used to be fairly rare in Pokhara but is nowadays regularly observed". *(PVDP)*

Broad Spark, Pokhara

8 Golden Sapphire, *Heliophorus brahma* Moore, 1858

In his 2011 guidebook to the butterflies of the Annapurna area, Colin described this one as a "most attractive" species. He listed it as "rare and local". It was first found in Nepal by the 1963 Japanese butterfly expedition in the Godavari area near Kathmandu, one of Colin's favourite "hunting grounds". Colin discovered it later in the Annapurna area. Nowadays, it flies along almost every stream in the southern part of the Annapurna Conservation Area and is fairly common. *(PVDP)*

Golden Sapphire, Lwang ACA

E Nymphalidae – Nymphalinae family – brush foots

9 **Annapurna Silverspot,** *Issoria (Kuekenthaliella) annapurnae Smith & Epstein* (an 'unavailable', manuscript name, not formally described).

'Officially', this is not a validly named species, because it has not yet been formally described. However, Colin noted it as a species in several publications. Hans Epstein recognized it as a new species and intended to describe it, but he did not get around to it. It differs from MacKinnon's

Annapurna Silverspot, Manang

Silverstripe mainly in size and probably in genitalia. Colin and Hans decided to call it *Kuekenthaliella annapurnae*. It still needs to be described. **(PVDP)**

10 Plain Tiger, Danaus chrysippus Linnaeus, 1758

11 Danaid Eggfly *Hypolimnas misippus* Linnaeus, 1764

Colin liked mimics and of all the mimics in Nepal, the Danaid Eggfly is the most perfect one. For beginners it is hard to differentiate between the female Danaid Eggfly and its model the Plain Tiger *Danaus chrysippus*. The male Danaid Eggfly did not feel a need to become a mimic and looks very different. Nymphalidae - Satyrinae **(PVDP)**

Plain Tiger *D*. Danaid Eggfly, Annapurna Eco-village, Astam

12 Nepal Wall, *Lopinga lehmanni* Forster, 1980

Colin discovered an unknown species of the Satyrinae in 1974 but was not allowed to take the only known specimen out of Nepal for identification and description. Several years later he caught more and took some specimens to the Natural History Museum in London. It was going to be described as *Lopinga annapurnae*. However, when Colin returned to Nepal, he found an article on his desk in which "his species" was described as *Crebeta lehmanni* (*Crebeta* is a synonym of *Lopinga*). Colin acknowledged that the Germans had caught their specimen one year earlier, so it was fair. And Colin could still give it its common name. ***(PVDP)***

Nepal Wall © Colin Smith

13 Himalayan Four-ring, *Ypthima parasakra* Eliot, 1987

Colin searched for two years for Hunnington's Four-ring. In the first year, he found a four-ring that he had not seen before. He sent some specimens to London and was told by John Eliot that this was not Hunnington's, but an altogether new species for science. Since it resembled *Ypthima sakra*, they called it *Ypthima parasakra*, Himalayan Four-ring. We saw quite a few Himalayan Four-rings on a recent survey in the Manang district of the Annapurna Conservation area. Colin found Hunnington's in the second year. *(PVDP)*

Himalayan Four-ring, Lower Mustang

14 Magpie Crow, *Euploea radamanthus* Fabricius, 1793

The Magpie Crow was listed for Nepal by Ramsay in 1867, and then it was not seen for more than a century. Most of Ramsay's observations were from Kathmandu, since Ramsay was a resident, he would be invited on Tiger hunts and would occasionally have been able to collect butterflies. Colin looked for it in east Nepal, but did not find it there. In 1990 Colin surveyed in Chitwan National Park and there, after 123 years, he found the Magpie Crow, where it turns out to be quite common.

Magpie Crow, from India

15 The Great Hockeystick Sailer, *Phaedyma aspasia* Fujioka, 1970

The subspecies is found only in Godavari and nowhere else, making it an extremely rare species. This striking butterfly was discovered in Godavari by the Japanese expedition of 1963 and has been recorded there on and off ever since. **(MSL)**

The Great Hockeystick Sailer Kathmandu

16 The Scarce Siren, *Hestina nicevillei* Moore, 1895

This is also only recorded from Godavari in Nepal and can be numerous on occasions. This species is also found in two other locations in India where it is extremely rare. **(MSL)**

Only found in central Nepal Kathmandu valley. It is recorded between 5,200-7,000 feet in May to June. It is one of the rarest butterflies in the world: described from a single specimen caught 150 years ago and only recorded in three localities. **(CS Butterflies of Nepal No 387)**

The Scarce Siren, Kathmandu

CHAPTER 8

Butterfly Audit of the Annapurna Conservation Area

Annapurna range early morning - Photo by P. Waine, 2022

Colin has been writing about butterflies since his first article in 1975 (*1975 Nature Conservation Society (28): Habits & Habitats of Nepal's Butterflies*) and has been collecting and displaying since 1967 at the Butterfly Museum in Pokhara. I wanted to cover what he did and the methods he used; however, having read a number of his books and articles, I realised this information was readily available. I did, however, want to explore one project that he did during his butterfly days. While on a visit to see him in October 2022, I went through some of his paperwork and discovered his notes on this project, which started in 2009, and culminated in a book being published of the work he carried out over 18 months.

Dear Mr Gurung,

Herewith a revised proposal for me to work with A.C.A.P., such as I discussed with you last month. As you suggested, I have addressed it to the National Trust for Nature Conservation and also made it a bit more general. (It need not be restricted only to photography of butterflies, although that is the area where I hope to be able to make the most significant contribution.)

As I explained, I do not require a regular salary. My UK pension (about a quarter of what most UK pensioners receive from the Government) is quite adequate to live on here, though vastly inadequate to live in any "Western" community! My only problem is how to stay in Nepal!

I enclose two copies of the letter, with the request that you please pass one on to the appropriate person in the National Trust for Nature Conservation with your recommendation for its serious consideration by them. I have put the date forward to June 1st as May is nearly here, and I can continue on a tourist visa till then.

Yours sincerely, Colin Smith

It was interesting to read that Colin's proposal to conduct this audit did not include a regular salary, and he was almost aged 73 when he started this survey. It occurred to me that you would need a certain passion to take on such a project, and a substantial personal motivation to drive you to complete it. Having seen this area, myself, while in Pokhara, it is challenging terrain, and each trip requires an expedition mentality and considerable physical and mental strength.

This project was started on 18th May 2009 and concluded on 18th November 2010. The booklet was published in 2011.

The Annapurna Conservation Area region covers an area of 7,629 square kilometres. It contains the world's deepest gorge and some of its highest peaks. It has two distinct climatic regions, 22 different forest types, 1,226 species of plants, 102 mammals, 488 birds, 40 reptiles and 23 amphibians, as well as 347 species of butterflies recorded to date (2009). *(This is a quote in the book by Lal*

Prasad Gurung, Project Director, NTNC - ACAP, Pokhara.) So, it is easy to see how this is such a fruitful place to spot butterflies. In comparison, the UK hosts 59 species.

Although Colin had visited the area before and taken many photos, the aim of this project was to start from scratch and take digital photographs. There were 330 different species recorded before this audit, and this would be his first set of digital photos taken in the area. Colin outlined some of the difficulties he would face in being able to achieve the aim of the project:

> *"The butterflies may be roughly divided into two groups:*
>
> *A) Palaearctic - flying at high altitudes (mostly in Mustang & Manang).*
> *B) The Oriental - at lower altitudes (in Kaski, Myagdi, Lamjung).*
>
> *The most difficult photos to obtain will be the high-altitude ones, since the areas are remote, and they only fly for a comparatively short season in the summer months."*

Colin started his contract at the beginning of May and spent the first couple of months setting himself up at the A.C.A.P. office and transferring his written butterfly database to his computer.

Trip One: 17th July 2009 to 29th July 2009

It is clear from his notes that Colin had to constantly think on his feet with the changes in weather, the lack of transport, and limited personnel to support him. For each trip he made, he sent a report which included the number of photos taken and the total number of different species.

From the pages of data he recorded for each trip, it would have taken up a lot of time to record and edit his photographs and write his report.

Having spoken to a number of staff at museums in the UK, it is clear that - even though Colin was self-taught - the professionalism with which he approached this project demonstrates his desire to learn and discover all he could on each of his expeditions.

Total number of photographs taken: 475
Total number of species recorded: 30

Trip Two: 11th August 2009 to 30th August 2009 – Manang Region

The trip was scheduled for 14 days. However, because of some of the known obstacles including access and the difficulty with transport, Colin took an extra six days to complete the trip.

He writes in his notes:

> "The 8.50 bus from Pokhara broke down before Demouli, and there was a two-hour delay to get it repaired, so we only reached Besishawr at 3.30 p.m. However, that still allowed us to get the (last) Bhulbhule bus at 4.40, which got there at 6.30.
>
> The ACAP office was very helpful and arranged a porter for us, costing 700 rupees per day, which was the same rate we had to pay in Mustang the next morning. We hoped to get there in three days, but because of the poor condition of the road only just made it in four."

Reading through Colin's notes, one gets the sense that on previous trips there had been a greater abundance of butterflies. Although he doesn't make a direct reference to what the issues may have been, he does notice that a number of the butterflies he found were higher up the mountains than before.

Colin observed in his report:

"Survey trips (for butterfly photos) at the highest altitudes need to be made in the summer months, as nearly all the butterflies found there fly almost exclusively between June and August.

The best weather is usually experienced there either in early June or in mid-August. Further survey trips should now be made at lower altitude, where the butterflies will continue flying throughout September, October and even into November.

I suggest that for these I use the ACAP Project Houses or Conservation Offices as bases and spend a few days at each, checking the local butterflies - particularly those at Ghorepani, Ghandruk, Lwang, Ghalekharka, Siklis, Yanjakhot and Bhujung."

Total number of photographs taken: 152
Total number of species recorded: 23

Trip Three: 13th September 2009 to 22nd September 2009

At the start of his report, Colin writes:

"Dear Sir,

Herewith the Preliminary Report of my trip (3) to Ghorepani, Ghandruk, and Lwang.

The idea of using the local ACAP offices as bases proved to be a sound one, but I need to have up-to-date information about those offices (as to where they are now situated!).

The butterflies were less than expected, but I still got some useful photos. It may be that the butterflies have been flying earlier in the season this year (perhaps due to global warming?).

Those at higher altitudes were very thin, but still, it should be worthwhile getting one more trip into lower altitudes between the Desain and Diwali holidays.

Yours sincerely, C. Smith"

When speaking with Dr Krushnamegh Kunte (from India) regarding Colin's work, he emphasised the importance of Colin's contributions, particularly his dedication to observing butterflies in the field to better understand their behaviour and record his findings.

Reading through Colin's notes, it is clear that his plan was to obtain the best possible results. He mentions on several occasions how staying another day or moving on to a new location was the right decision. He sent monthly reports to update and propose alternative strategies where he felt they would add value to the project as a whole.

Total number of photographs taken: 627

**Total number of species recorded:
48 (30 of which had not been recorded previously)**

**Trip Four: 6th October 2009 to
15th October 2009 – Lamjung District**

Colin writes:

"As the seasons progress, the butterflies tend to be more abundant at lower altitudes. About the lowest altitude in

the A.C.A. occurs in Lamjung – in the Bhulbhule region, where you can get down to 800m."

Total number of photographs taken: 302
Total number of species recorded: 33

Colin made a note in his report about the state of the habitat:

"On other treks I have complained that the making of roads is destroying (at least the more accessible) habitat for butterflies. But on this occasion, it is the natural forces (river erosion) that is doing so.

However, there are still good places – particularly the wooded sections before Chansu and the paths over the bridge from where good habitat remains.

For this trip we were very much limited to the lower altitudes, but on future surveys, when the butterflies fly higher, there could be many 'village' paths to explore if we had more time available.

However, we now have nearly 130 photos of low-altitude butterflies (plus the 20 high-altitude ones), so we have made a good start for our future publication."

Trip Five: 20th October 2009 to 22nd October 2009 – Chansu, Kaski Region

Colin writes in his report:

"There were still a couple of dozen reasonably common low-altitude butterflies that should be out this time of year, that I hadn't got photographs of in this area of the A.C.A., so I wanted to take the opportunity while I still had time to do so."

Total number of photographs taken: 449
Total number of species recorded: 19

These were the last trips of 2009. In his monthly report, Colin summarised his data to date:

"We have been making new records - e.g. the Mustang trip added one new species, and the Manang trip four new species to the original list of recorded 330 species, but the low-altitude trips since then have added more.

In all, I have taken over 2,000 photos - first in Mustang-Manang (20 species not found elsewhere), and later in Kaski-Lamjung (130 species found generally across the area, though some being local)."

Trip Six: 23rd March 2010 to 29th March 2010 - Bhujung

The first trip of 2010 took place at the end of March to Bhujung. Having never been to the area before, this was Colin's first opportunity to take photographs. He says in his report that the butterflies, on the whole, were very thin and suggests that they may appear later in the year.

Total number of photographs taken: 241
Total number of species recorded: 48

(Of which seven were new species for Bhujung - bringing the Bhujung list from 159 species to 166. Of these, 77 had now been photographed.)

Trip Seven: 29th April 2010 to 5th May 2010 - Myagdi & Kaski (Sikha & Ghandruk)

Total number of photographs taken: 298
Total number of species recorded: 66

(Of which 36 were new to the area)

Trip Eight: 25th May 2010 to 30th May 2010 – Lwang

The original plan was to include Siklis; however, it was not possible to conduct them together. During this trip, Colin was keen to capture a photo of a Mottled Argus (previously spotted in 2001). Unfortunately, he was unable to spot it. However, he did take a photo of a Krishna Peacock - one of Nepal's rarest butterflies.

In his notes, he records:

> *"It is particularly hard to get a picture of this butterfly as it has only a very short flying season – roughly the last week in May and first week of June. We only saw it once (briefly)."*

Total number of photographs taken: 421
Total number of species recorded: 52

Colin spent the following months working on the layout of his book. He proposed that it be printed in a similar format to another guidebook themed on birds, which used a pocket-sized vertical layout. Colin wanted the book to be useful for identifying butterflies but also practical and easy to carry and use in the field.

The book was finally published in 2011. However, only 1,000 copies were printed. Considering the number of visitors to this region of Nepal, there may well have been scope for a second print.

CHAPTER 9

Quest for Citizenship

Colin's desire was that someday he would be a citizen of Nepal. Since the passing of his parents in the UK and his brother relocating to New Zealand, he felt there was nothing to go back to England for.

As a visitor in Nepal, he was constantly having to reapply for visas to prolong his stay. In the early days, this would mean a trip to Kathmandu and all the expense associated with each application.

Colin first applied to become a Nepali citizen in 1994. Unfortunately, there were government elections, and he feared that his application became a low priority. In his letters, he states the reasons for wanting to become a citizen. One purpose was to dispense with the constant visa applications, which were costing about $20 a month, plus the time it took to travel to Kathmandu. Citizenship would allow him to travel more freely within Nepal. He also wished to be able to purchase a plot of land and build a house.

Colin's quest to become a citizen had been ongoing, making a number of approaches to various authorities. He even decided that if he were to marry a Nepali woman, this might also help the process. So, on the 25th of July 2008, Colin got married to a Nepalese lady and provided a home for her. He remained married and provided his wife with a better standard of living and higher status within society, although they didn't live together.

A number of his local friends started an online campaign for Colin to become a citizen, although this did not lead to much officially at this point.

In 2018, Colin writes in his journal:

> *"I have been trying to obtain Nepali citizenship (as I intend to spend the rest of my life here). I have gone through all the procedures with the local administration, submitted documents from all the organisations I have worked for, been vetted by the police, had hospital checks (on my mental and physical health). I got five local residents to*

vouch for me and sent it all via the Chief District Officer to Kathmandu.

There remains only one thing, and that is to renounce my British citizenship. To do this, I have the required forms but must either have already obtained that of another country or have an official letter from that country confirming I will be given it once my renunciation is submitted. I am waiting for such a letter. (As far as I can tell, Nepal has never given such a letter to anyone.)

There is one other possibility, and that would be to be given just 'Honorary Citizenship', for which you do not have to give up your own. As far as I can make out, Nepal has given this to two persons only: Edmund Hillary (of New Zealand) for not only climbing Everest but his work in schools for Sherpa children, and Toni Hagen (of Switzerland) for his work travelling all over Nepal and writing on its wildlife. (He chaired an international conference on this here in 1994.)

But I do not know that my work on butterflies compares with these.

However, now I have been getting much publicity - newspaper articles and appearances on television - and many have said that I should be granted citizenship.

But that counted for little until two television producers who were interviewing me said, 'Why don't you contact Baburam Bhattarai, whom you taught in Luitel in 1968?'

He happened to be in Pokhara for a meeting at the time, so they took me down to see him, and I actually spoke to him for about five minutes. He promised to do what he could for me, but it would need an act of Parliament!

So that's the position to date."

In his letter, Colin is modest about all his work on Nepali butterflies:

"No, the thing I like most are the Nepali people. Not just a few in high positions, but ordinary village folk, living on a shoestring budget, working hard to make two ends meet. Often visited by disasters (floods, landslides, shortages of essential supplies, to say nothing of lightning strikes or earthquakes, or accidents), as I have lived here myself with whom I can empathise!

This is why I want to be a Nepali citizen, and live the rest of my life here, and die here, and have my ashes thrown into the Seti River."

To Government of Nepal

Why I desire to have Citizenship of Nepal

Dear Sir,

It is not easy to give just one simple answer.

There are many reasons-

(1) **HABIT** I am a creature of habit. I have lived in 4 or 5 Countries of the World, but none so much as in Nepal, where I have spent over 52 years (more than half my life!

(2) I was born in England, and brought up there, but not being particularly gifted, soon saw that I could be more use to a third-world country than to U.K. and the final choice of that country came to Nepal..

(3) All my close Relatives in U.K. are dead or have left the country. (I still have friends there are keep in touch be e-mail. They would no doubt welcome me as a Visitor, but to stay for the rest of my life is quite another matter!)

(4) I have a brother in New Zealand, who would welcome me, but here his Government would not. (As a Tourist for 6 months, Yes. But to spend the rest of my life there, That would be another matter. If I was young with something to contribute to the Country, maybe, but being and old Crock (*in Hospital 3 times in2017*) and likely to need medical attention, definitely No!)

(5) Some people would imagine it is for the sake of **Nepal's Butterflies**, But New Guinea has interesting butterflies, so do many other places too.

(6) Or the views of the highest Mountains of the World, or other wild-life, or pleasant climate ,**all of which I appreciate**.

(7) No the thing I like most are the Nepali people!

Not just a few in high positions, but the ordinary village folk, living on a shoe-string budget, working hard to make two ends meet., often visited by disasters (floods, land-slides, shortages of essential supplies, to say nothing of lightning strikes or earth-quakes, or accidents), as I have lived here myself, **with whom I cam empathize!**

That is why I would like to be a **NEPALI Citizen,** and live the rest of my life here, and die here, and have my ashes thrown into the Sheti river.

Yours sincerely.

Colin Smith.

C. Smith 24 07 2018

Colin's copy of letter sent to Nepali government - July 2018

Meanwhile, back in the UK, having followed the online publicity about Colin's quest, I sat down with Surendra, and he began to reconnect with his contacts in Nepal and the UK to champion this cause. It was clear that we would have to try and petition as many people as possible, and as high up as possible, in the present government. During this time I received an email from the Nepali Embassy in London.

9th August 2019 – Request from the Nepal Embassy in London

Dear Peter,

Greetings from the Embassy of Nepal. We would be grateful if you could kindly provide the details of important work and contributions at the national and international level by Colin Philip Smith.

Thank you.

27th August 2019 – My response:

Dear Sirs,

Thank you for giving me time to put this together. Although I haven't seen Colin for some while, I recently became aware that he was requesting to become a Nepal citizen.

A friend of mine, Surendra Bahadur Shrestha, brought this to my attention. Since that time, I have been trying to put some information together which I feel will support Colin Smith's application.

I have put some documents together which I believe provide strong supporting evidence for Colin to become a citizen of Nepal.

The first document is a curriculum vitae, which outlines a timeline of Colin's activities and reflects the time Colin has been dwelling in Nepal. The last page includes dates as shown on his passport.

During his time in Nepal, Colin pursued his love of butterflies, which has culminated in a number of collections he has set up - and, in doing so, attained the nickname, Putali Baje.

The second document, titled Putali Baje, *outlines his contribution to the butterfly collection. The third document is a copy of a letter that Colin Smith wrote in 2018. The fourth is a certificate of appreciation from EGBOSA.*

I hope you can take a look at the attached documents – I believe they make a strong case for Colin Smith's application.

Very kind regards, Peter Waine

Surendra Shrestha explains the steps he and his contacts took to promote Colin's quest to become a citizen of Nepal:

"In Nepal, Colin was affectionately known as *Putali Baje*, or the Butterfly Grandpa, for dedicating his life to studying and teaching about Nepal's diverse butterfly species. His final wish was to die in Pokhara, be cremated, and have his ashes scattered in the Seti River. Despite being a devout Christian, he chose cremation over burial to avoid wasting fertile land. Another wish was to die as a Nepali citizen.

Since the 1990s, he had made several attempts to acquire Nepali citizenship, even petitioning when his student, Baburam Bhattarai, became Prime Minister. However, for reasons unknown, he never succeeded.

This situation troubled me deeply. While anyone legally residing more than ten years in a country like the UK can acquire citizenship, why couldn't someone who had spent his entire life in Nepal, contributed extensively to its education and biodiversity, and abandoned his British citizenship, become Nepali?

Colin had played a pivotal role in Nepal's education system, contributing to schools like Gandaki Boarding and Tribhuvan University, and had established a museum to showcase Nepal's rich biodiversity, collecting over 600 butterfly species from across the country.

Despite his contributions, Colin's request for Nepali citizenship went unanswered for over 50 years. This felt unjust, and I decided to act. I reached out to Chandra Bahadur Rokahaji, a former advisor to the Non-Resident Nepali Association (NRNA) based in Pokhara, and connected with Surendra Pariyar, a close associate of Colin. Kapildev Thapa, an NRNA member from Japan, was also in Nepal at the time and agreed to assist.

With Kapil's support, we engaged the then Minister of Home Affairs, Ram Bahadur Thapa 'Badal', and Dr Prem Ale. After visiting Colin, Kapil confirmed the urgency of his condition and pushed for action. Surendra Pariyar helped submit the necessary documents to the Ministry of Home Affairs. Due to Colin's declining health, the process was expedited, and the Cabinet decided to grant him honorary Nepali citizenship.

This was made possible through the support of several key individuals, including Ran Bahadur Thapa (former ward chairman), Chandra Bahadur Buda (Chief District Officer), and Arun Sapkota (Ministry of Home Affairs). Colin's students Bishnu Dev Parai and Sunil Ulak played vital roles in the process.

The contributions of others – like Raj Kumar Gurung (Annapurna Conservation Area Project), Raju Acharya (Nature Friends), and Arjun Acharya (Minister of Tourism's secretary) – were also essential in making this happen. With the efforts of all these dedicated individuals, Colin's wish to be recognised as a Nepali citizen was finally fulfilled, honouring his immense dedication to Nepal's education, environment, and biodiversity."

On the 2nd of December 2019, after verifying the required paperwork through the British Embassy, Colin Smith was granted honorary Nepali citizenship.

Since Colin's presentation, the same honour has been granted to Um Hong-Gil, a South Korean philanthropist – making four recipients in total.

Colin receiving his Honorary Citizenship Certificate in Kathmandu - Photo: The Himalayan Times

Reported in the press:

Southern Asia Times - 24th November 2019

Kathmandu - British national Colin Smith, known as *Putali Baje*, is set to get an honorary citizenship certificate of Nepal.

A Cabinet meeting held on 15th November had decided to grant honorary citizenship to Smith, who has been living in Nepal for a long time. The Ministry of Home Affairs had recommended citizenship for him based on documents submitted by Smith. Citizenship and National ID Card Management Officer Arun Sapkota said Smith would be granted citizenship as per the government decision, *The Himalayan Times* reported.

"The federal Cabinet can issue honorary citizenship. Earlier, such citizenship was granted to two foreign nationals. The Home Ministry will prepare the required procedure and issue the citizenship certificate," said Sapkota.

The constitution has stipulated that the government can grant honorary citizenship to a foreign national of international reputation.

Smith had come to Nepal through the United Mission in 1966 to teach. He is 83 years old. Smith taught maths and science at Gorkha's Amarjyoti Secondary School. Former Prime Minister Baburam Bhattarai and Doctor Upendra Devkota were his students. Smith is also a renowned butterfly expert.

Himalayan News Service – Published 3rd December 2019 at 3:45 p.m.

Putali Baje obliged with Nepali citizenship

Following a long wait, British national Colin Philip Smith, popularly known as *Putali Baje*, has finally managed to obtain a Nepali citizenship certificate.

The Home Ministry's Citizenship and National Identity Card Management Department provided the certificate to Smith in Kathmandu today.

Section Officer Arun Sapkota handed the document, with registration number 01/076/077, to the foreign national who has long been residing in Pokhara, ever since he retired as a United Mission teacher.

Earlier, a Cabinet meeting on 15th November had decided to oblige the British national, who spent a long time researching butterflies in Nepal, with honorary citizenship. "He was obliged with an honorary citizenship as per the Cabinet decision," said the Section Officer.

Among the students he taught were former Prime Minister Baburam Bhattarai and the late senior Dr Upendra

Devkota. He taught them science and maths at Amarjyoti Secondary School in Gorkha.

Smith lives in Gyarjati of Pokhara Metropolis-18, where he had bought a plot of land in the name of one of his Nepali acquaintances, who had worked with him for quite a long time. The citizenship certificate provided to him includes the address of his residence.

After the government introduced the provision to provide honorary citizenship to persons of international stature in its Citizenship Act 2063, Colin became the third person to receive such an honour.

What is Honorary Citizenship?

Honorary citizenship is a status bestowed by a city or government on a foreign or native individual whom it considers to be especially admirable or otherwise worthy of the distinction. The honour is usually symbolic and does not confer any change to citizenship or nationality. (3a)

Honorary citizenship was included in the Nepal Citizenship Act 1964:

Article 6A – Conferment of Honorary Nepali Citizenship

(1) Notwithstanding anything contained in Section 6, His Majesty may grant honorary Nepali citizenship on the recommendation of His Majesty's Government to any person who has gained special reputation.

(2) The person who has been granted honorary citizenship under Sub-section (1) shall have the same status as a naturalised Nepali citizen.

How common is honorary citizenship in Nepal? The list is not large – in fact, it totals four.

Others who were granted Honorary Citizenship of Nepal

Toni Hagen (17 August 1917 – 18 April 2003) awarded Nepali citizenship 1995

Dr Hagen was the first foreigner to trek throughout Nepal during geological and geographic survey work and mapping on behalf of the United Nations. He walked over 14,000 km, walking several times across Nepal, where the topography is mostly hilly to snow-covered. He filmed Nepalese cultural and ethnic diversity originally as produced as a silent documentary, and later with an English narration in his own voice.

Sir Edmund Percival Hillary (20 July 1919 - 11 January 2008) awarded Nepali citizenship 29 May 2003

Edmund Hillary was a New Zealand mountaineer, explorer, and philanthropist. On 29 May 1953, Hillary and Sherpa mountaineer Tenzing Norgay became the first climbers confirmed to have reached the summit of Mount Everest. They were part of the ninth British expedition to Everest, led by John Hunt. From 1985 to 1988 he served as New Zealand's High Commissioner to India and Bangladesh and concurrently as Ambassador to Nepal.

Um Hong Gil 4 September 1960 - present) awarded Nepali citizenship 19 January 2020

Minister of Communications and Information Technology Gokul Prasad Baskota provided the honorary citizenship certificate to South Korean philanthropist Um Hong Gil amidst a function very recently on 13 January 2020. He has established the Um Hong Gil Human Foundation in 2009, with 15 model schools being built in 12 districts, with two more schools being built in Kathmandu.

CHAPTER 10

Meeting Colin and Seeing Nepal

On the 8th of October 2022, I landed in Kathmandu - a vibrant and busy place. I immediately started to like it. My first stop was a brief stay at the Kathmandu Guest House, situated in the middle of the Thamel district. This was recommended by a friend at work. The contrast between the busy streets surrounding the hotel and the quiet, tranquil setting inside was remarkable.

The shops and streets were just what I had expected: the hustle and bustle of the locals' daily lives; narrow lanes full of colour from fabrics hanging outside the shops; and a background of constant chatter from food outlets. That first night, I simply sat in the garden to slowly take in the smells, sounds, and atmosphere that made this such a perfect place to begin my journey.

The following day, I was met by a friend of Surendra Shrestha - Kapil Dev Thapa - and had the pleasure of visiting some of the many ancient temples. It brought to mind Colin's comment when he first arrived in Nepal:

> *"The thing that impresses you is the carving and the shrines. Truly, Kathmandu has more temples than houses and more gods than people."*

What an introduction to Nepal. We had a glorious day, and I was in awe of the beauty and heritage that still stands. Kathmandu opens one's eyes to cultures we're unfamiliar with in the West. It would take a much longer visit to truly appreciate the richness of the place.

In 1966, when Colin first arrived in Nepal, it must have been an even greater contrast to where he had travelled from in the United Kingdom. Colin's favourite place in the whole of Nepal is Pokhara. However, he visited Kathmandu over the years for many reasons, including visas, working on the publishing of some of his books, and for healthcare. He recorded his first impression in 1966:

> *"Kathmandu Valley is saucer-shaped, 4,000 feet up in the middle of the Mahabharat range of hills. The mountains*

around it are about 9,000 feet high, with streams (mostly piped for water) running down into the valley.

The valley floor is mostly rice fields, with a few brick factories. When the mud becomes too poor to grow rice, they dig it out and turn it into bricks - and grow rice two feet lower down. They have 70 feet of mud, since the valley used to be a lake. Most of the houses are brick-built.

It has three main cities, and when I went there the total population was about one million. Local transport was by cycle-rickshaw or by Tiger Taxi. There were just two bus routes out of the city; hiring bicycles was a convenient way to get about. It had mains electricity; milk and bread were available."

When I arrived in Nepal, it felt like a fascinating country - and the fact that the British didn't occupy it when they were in India means it remains very authentic. The streets of Kathmandu are incredibly busy. Traffic seems to have its own rules, which I assume comply with some form of regulation. In what appears to be absolute chaos, everyone is careful and polite - none of the open frustration you often see on UK roads back home.

Two days later, on the 10th, I took an internal flight to Pokhara and was met at the airport by Surendra Pariyar.

Surendra now manages the Butterfly Museum in Pokhara and became my guide for the duration of my stay. We sat on a low wall in the car park of Pokhara airport, and he produced a small notebook in which he had written out my itinerary for the coming days.

I could see that he had made a huge effort to make my stay as worthwhile as possible, and we became good friends. Instead of using a taxi, I'd share the back of his scooter as he drove around the various places, he had arranged for me to visit. My transport from the airport had been with Dr Ananda Shrestha and his SUV - the brother of my friend in the UK, Surendra Shrestha. Fortunately, there was no need to attempt to fit me and my suitcases on the back of Surendra's scooter!

Our first stop was to visit Colin at the Green Pastures Hospital, in their Palliative Care Unit. When we met, I gave him some traditional English shortbread and sweets, which I thought would be appreciated! He was being looked after by the staff and by Dr Ruth Powys, the head of the Palliative Care Unit. I became quite friendly with Ruth and the senior nurse, Manju - the Palliative Care Coordinator.

The joy on Colin's face at my visit was appreciated by all the staff. I was the first relative of Colin to visit him for many years and the overall mood was one of tranquillity.

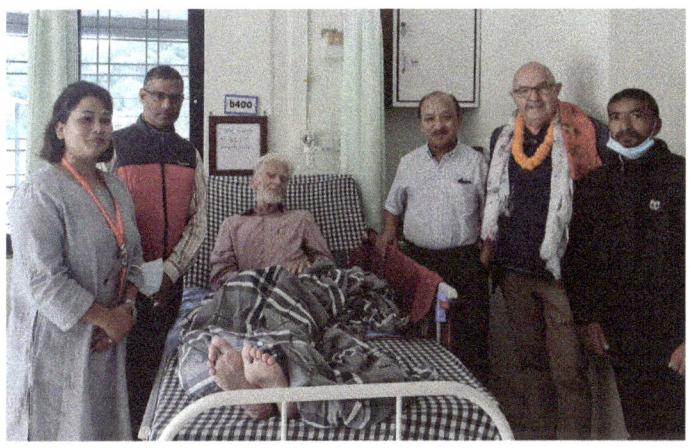

Group photo, left to right: Manju, Surendra Pariyar, Colin Smith, Ananda Shrestha, myself, and Min Pariyar (Colin's carer)

It was while with him at the Green Pastures Medical Centre that I met (for the first time) Min Bahadur Pariyar, who as a young boy in Pokhara many years earlier, had met Colin. Min became interested in collecting butterflies, and in the process, the two formed a deep bond. Min has been by Colin's side for 36 years, accompanying him on many of his forays into the wild. It is Min's family who have been helping Colin for more than 25 years.

Green Pastures was established in 1957 by the International Nepal Fellowship as a leprosy mission and became a hospital in 1970. Colin had visited Green Pastures many times over the years and was well known and loved by the staff.

Green Pastures was very different to what I expected, with a beautiful outdoor sensory garden near to Colin's ward. Min was also able to stay at the hospital and assisted Colin in taking short walks in the grounds.

On a second visit to see Colin, with the help of the staff, we were able to set up a Zoom meeting so that Colin could see and speak to his brother Arnold and his niece Kate in New Zealand.

During this visit, Dr Ruth Powys spoke with me about Colin's health. Although Colin still needed to be supported, he no longer required the intensive care he had been receiving at the hospital.

She took me to Aged Care Centre, a supported living unit nearby, which she felt could be the next step for Colin. Min would be able to accompany him, and he would be looked after by the house parents - a couple responsible for running the supported living unit. The unit is within the grounds of a Christian church, which would offer him additional fellowship. The unit seemed very suitable; however, Ruth explained that Colin's wish was to stay in the hospital or go home. She spoke with me, as his relative, to see if we could persuade Colin to move in - with the understanding that he would be readmitted to the Green Pastures Medical Centre should his health deteriorate.

Not long after I flew back to the UK, Colin moved to the care centre, and over the ensuing months, he was readmitted twice more to the hospital.

During my stay in Pokhara, I was able to visit him twice more at the hospital. Meeting and chatting with Colin was important in helping me understand him better. The conversations were not long, as he was frail, but I felt it was important to have met with him in Nepal. My only regret is that my original plan to visit Colin in 2020 had been cancelled due to COVID. At that time, Colin's health and long-term memory were much better. There were quite a few questions he would have been able to answer or recall - information about the butterflies that had consumed him during his time in Nepal.

I then spent the next few days travelling around Pokhara, meeting the people who had been part of Colin's life. I visited the old neighbourhood where he had once rented a room, the Christian church he attended in Pokhara, and the Prithvi Narayan Campus where the Butterfly Museum is located. I even met the first principal of the college, Mr George John.

All the people I met spoke about Colin with great fondness and respect for the work he had accomplished in Nepal. It was clear that Colin, in his own way, had made a lasting impression - and his footprints were everywhere.

Surendra had invited me to witness the sunrise from a viewing platform over Pokhara and informed me that he would have to pick me up at 05:30 the following morning. Despite the early start, I was not disappointed, and the magnificent sight will stay with me forever. We had breakfast at the viewpoint - it must be one of the best locations anywhere in the world.

Everywhere I went, I was received with friendship, generosity, and openness by the people I met. The scenery was stunning, and even parts of Kathmandu left one with the feeling that it is a very special place, rich with tradition and history. I now understand why Colin grew to see Nepal as the place where he belonged - where he could spend his time observing and recording the natural beauty that surrounded him.

CHAPTER 11

A Fitting Farewell

After my visit in October 2022, I kept in contact with Green Pastures Hospital and with Kate and Grant in New Zealand. Colin's health seemed to fluctuate, but he transferred to the Aged Care Centre at Nayagaun Church, which was only a short distance from Green Pastures and the place Dr Ruth had taken me to while I was in Nepal. Over the following months, he would return to Green Pastures whenever his health deteriorated.

We also had three Zoom meetings which included Kate and Grant with their boys James and Sam, plus Arnold, his brother. It was during one of these Zoom calls that I remember Colin and Arnold reminiscing about the mischief they used to get up to as boys. It was a joy to see, and to know that for both of them, these conversations may not have happened had they not got back in touch.

I was moved by the care and kindness of all the staff at Green Pastures and the Aged Care Centre. I know it's their job to care, but I feel that Colin had been adopted over the years as a member of their extended family. To see him at peace and so well cared for was a great comfort. They had even accommodated Min, who had been caring for him, and he had almost become part of the team looking after Colin in his final year.

Although not entirely surprising, it was with great sadness that I received the following emails:

Friday 3rd November 2023, 19:39 – Email from Dr Ruth Powys

Head of Palliative Care Unit, Green Pastures Hospital, International Nepal Fellowship

Dear Kate and all,

Colin was readmitted to the unit in late August after a short time back at the Aged Care Centre, as he refused to eat, drink, or allow Min to look after him properly.

He improved a bit with extra support and gentle encouragement, and although he has remained very frail, he had been stable. However, he has significantly deteriorated since yesterday.

As per his wishes, we are keeping him comfortable, and Min is aware of the very poor prognosis.

The Mayor of Pokhara had wanted to visit Colin and apparently turned up late today, and Dr Amrita was there. They want to honour Colin. Dr Amrita wasn't sure Colin understood much of what was happening, as he has minimal response at present.

Nayagaun Church leadership are aware of Colin's current situation and deterioration, and they visited him again this afternoon.

I will be leaving Pokhara on 24th November and going back to Australia.

Warm regards, Ruth

Saturday 4th November 2023, 04:41 – Email from Dr Ruth Powys

Dear all,

Colin peacefully died in the unit this morning at 03:00 hours. A remarkable life, lived with dignity to the end, and now he is with His Lord.

Nayagaun Church are aware, and as per Colin's wishes, there will be arrangements made in collaboration with Nadipur Church for his funeral today.

I will update you.

Warm regards, Ruth

Saturday 4th November 2023, 12:23 – Email from Dr Ruth Powys

Dear all,

The funeral will now be on Monday morning at 10 a.m. at Nadipur Church - where Colin was a member for so many years.

Normally, funerals happen very quickly in Nepal (usually the same morning), but the Pokhara Mayor wanted to honour Colin with a police guard salute and Nepali flag.

However, as there was a significant earthquake last night in western Nepal - with deaths and casualties - the mayor was urgently called to Kathmandu today for meetings on the government's immediate disaster response. He has requested we wait until Monday.

This is not a problem, as we have a small mortuary room here at the PCCD unit, and it is easier for both churches. Today being Saturday already involves a busy programme for both churches with services, etc.

After preparing the casket, we will have a short service at PCCD at 9 a.m. on Monday, where many of the staff will be able to attend. Then the vehicle and casket will go to Nadipur Church.

We can capture some photos and hopefully some video. Zooming is probably not an option.

Please do send on a message and I can read it out at the PCCD service and pass it on to the Nadipur leaders for the main service.

Warm regards, Ruth

Summary of the Funeral for Colin Philip Smith – by Dr Ruth Powys (Russell)

Colin died at 03:00 hours on Saturday 4th November 2023 (in Nepal: 19th of Kartik 2080; 2080/07/19). The funeral for Colin - *Putali Baje* (Butterfly Grandfather) - was held on Monday 6th November, and took place in three parts.

Part 1 - Green Pastures Medical Centre

In the early morning, representatives from both Nayagaun and Nadipur churches came to the Palliative Care Unit and, together with the staff and Min, prepared the casket and body. Colin was buried wearing a *Dhaka topi* (traditional Nepali hat), as he always wore a *topi* when out, and a lovely butterfly T-shirt that had been his favourite (he had it made some years ago). The staff specially had a new copy made. As per custom, part of the top of the casket was left open during the funeral for people to see the face, pay their respects, and place flowers or tributes on the casket.

With many staff and friends gathered, we held a half-hour service under a large outdoor area. Some of Colin's favourite hymns were sung or played, including *The King of Love My*

Shepherd Is. Elders from Nayagaun Church led the service, with assistance from Nadipur Church, and a few members of the Palliative Care team shared about Colin's life and their memories of him. Min sat close to the casket. His family was mentioned by name, along with some early history.

We shared some of the things that Colin had told us over the years about what mattered most to him. We read his favourite verse - 2 Timothy 1:12b-13:

> "... But I am not ashamed, for I know whom I have believed, and am sure that he is able to guard until that Day what has been entrusted to me."

Dr Amrita also shared that just the day before, she had shown Colin an article recently published about his life in one of the airline magazines and prayed with him.

Part 2 - Journey to the Butterfly Museum

As the casket was placed on the decorated vehicle to begin the next phase, the *Hallelujah Chorus* was played. Colin had frequently told us in recent years how much he looked forward to being with Jesus and singing the *Hallelujah Chorus* with all the angels and saints. We rejoice that he is now doing just that.

There was then a procession heading to north Pokhara and the PN Campus. Those closest to Colin travelled on the back of the truck with his body, and a large picture of Colin was displayed on the front of the vehicle. This was followed by a cavalcade of motorcycles and a few taxis and cars. Together, they made their way up to Nadipur, to the PN Campus and the Annapurna Natural History Museum - where the Butterfly Museum is located.

Part 3 – The Service and Speeches

The next official part of the service took place outside the Butterfly Museum building. The Mayor had organised this, and there was a police guard and many important attendees. At least six speeches were given, including from the Mayor, the current head of the PN Campus, the oldest surviving and most revered academic who had worked with Colin, former students, local government representatives, and senior figures from Gandaki Boarding School and various other organisations. This part of the service lasted around an hour.

The Mayor shared how, on Friday afternoon, he had gone to the PCCD Unit to see Colin. Even though Colin was very weak and barely responsive, the Mayor was able to tell him how much he was appreciated. Colin gave a small smile and tried to place his hands together in a *Namaste* – a moment that was very special to all present.

People placed flowers on the casket. It was then draped with a PN Campus cloth and the Nepali flag – an immense honour. Gandaki Boarding School also contributed their cloth, which was placed beneath the national flag. Various important individuals laid their official tributes.

There were two banners with Colin's picture on either side of the museum entrance, and another banner showing different moments from his life. These included Colin with Arnold and his parents, a young girl assumed to be Kate, early photos with students at Gandaki Boarding School, and pictures outside his house.

People from Nadipur Church sang Nepali songs that Colin loved, and the head of the Pokhara Christian Community led a prayer.

The casket was then placed back on the truck. Because of time constraints, it was decided to go directly to the northern burial site used by the churches and hold the main Christian service there, rather than first going to Nadipur Church.

It was a truly remarkable day of honouring Colin and all that he had done and contributed to Nepal. It clearly showed how deeply *Putali Baje* is respected and remembered in this country.

The hearse being prepared to leave PN Campus.
Photo Ruth Powys 2023

CHAPTER 12

Last Reflections

On his trips back to the UK in the late 1990s and early 2000s, Colin was given a few contracts at various museums, where he was asked to inspect existing collections and either amend or verify the data. At the National Museums Liverpool, he catalogued over 50,000 specimens. At Bolton Museum, it was a much smaller collection. At Sheffield Museums Trust, he reviewed their holdings - some of which he and his brother Arnold had donated from their own collection, along with a private collection they had inherited, containing approximately 7,000 specimens of butterflies.

I was fortunate to visit these museums and talk to people who had worked with Colin at Liverpool and Bolton, and I spoke to a colleague at Sheffield who now curates the entomology department. The displays in the cabinets look amazing - even without any prior knowledge of the butterfly world, it was incredible to see so many different specimens.

The Perception of Others

I felt it was important to find out the views of these professionals regarding the importance of the contribution Colin's work has made to the knowledge of the diverse world of butterflies and moths of Nepal.

Alistair McLean, Curator of Natural Science, Sheffield Museums Trust:

"Lots of people were collecting butterflies at the time, but comparatively few recorded the detail that Colin did, making his observations instantly more useful and scientifically important.

The notion of recording the wildlife of an area goes back a long way, but the more systematic approach adopted by Colin was comparatively new (biological record centres, which record this kind of information, were only founded in the 1960s). Colin clearly knew his stuff, and his contributions to Sheffield

Museum - in terms of both his expertise and specimens - are considerable.

I think it's safe to say that Colin's contribution to Lepidoptery in Nepal cannot be overstated, both in terms of his research into its biodiversity, but also in popularising the notion of recording wildlife in the region."

Dr Steve Judd, Senior Curator (Entomology), National Museums Liverpool:

"He was clearly a pioneer, and I guess that he regarded Nepal as his adopted home and felt that the collection belonged there - which it did.

He was undoubtedly an outstanding authority on Nepalese and Himalayan butterflies generally. He was much more than a collector, and I think that the urge to collect was probably secondary.

I believe his prime motivation was to understand more about their biology and distribution in order to help protect and conserve them."

Steve Garland, Senior Keeper of Natural History, Bolton Museum (during Colin's visit to the UK in the 1990s):

"It is impressive that he kept accurate records of the species and the localities where he saw them. Bearing in mind this is pre-mobile phone and pre-portable GPS - and I remember when we trekked in Nepal in 1985, the maps left a lot to be desired.

His work didn't just list the species in the country but identified the areas of Nepal where they occurred - which is an achievement. A lot of museum collections just have labels saying things like 'India' or 'Nepal', which are of limited value. His are much more valuable as they include better location data - which underpinned his publications.

So many people from Europe collected material overseas and then returned with it to their home country. It was very forward-thinking for Colin to realise how much more valuable his collecting and recording would be if it remained in Nepal and was then available to future local butterfly researchers and recorders.

It is also significant that he didn't collect for his personal desire to collect, but with the aim of furthering both the knowledge of - and to encourage future interest in - Nepal's butterflies. The displays of specimens are an important part of this too, giving visitors a chance to see some of the material - and hopefully foster interest in butterflies."

Colin's contribution to the displays in the UK museums was important at the time and still today provides a valuable resource. Colin was at home among butterflies, wherever they were. I understand now that what started as a hobby when he was a young boy had become his *raison d'être*, and the driving force behind the work he completed in Nepal.

CHAPTER 13

Published works

Butterfly Articles and Publications by Colin P. Smith (1975-2018)

(A) Articles in Scientific Journals

Year	Published under	Title
1975	Nature Conservation Society (28)	Habits & Habitats of Nepal's Butterflies
1976	Nature Conservation Society (29)	Butterflies of far West Nepal
	Jour. N.H.M. 1 p.71- 81	Some interesting Butterflies of E. Nepal (pts.1 &2) (listing 25 species)
	Jour. N.H.M. 1 p.143- 150	Some Butterflies of W. Nepal - part 1 (Spring) (listing 4 species)

1978	Jour. N.H.M. 2 p.127-185	Scientific list of Nepal's Butterflies (listing 567 species)
1979	Jour. N.H.M. 3 p.151-158	Interesting Butterflies of E. Nepal (pts.3 &.4) (listing 22 species)
	Jour. N.H.M. 3 p.159-164	Corrections to Scientific List of Butterflies (listing 19 species)
1980	Nat. Hist. Museum, Kathmandu	Commoner Butterflies of Nepal (listing 100 Genera)
1977	Jour. N.H.M. 1 p.68-70	Some interesting Butterflies of Godavari (listing 2 species)
	Jour. N.H.M. 4 p.41-53	Some Butterflies of W. Nepal part 2 (Summer) (listing 16 species)
	Jour. N.H.M. 4 p.127-129	Further changes to Nepal List of Butterflies (total to 592)
	Nat. Hist. Museum, Kathmandu bull.2	Field-guide to Nepal's Butterflies (listing 480 species)
1983	Jour. Bombay N.H.S. 80(1) p.166-170	Three new subspecies of Butterflies from Nepal 2

Published works

1995	Nepal Biodiversity Profiles	Red Data Book Status Reports of Butterfly Species (listing 142 species)
2004	Bionotes, ALIGARH No.6 p.3-5, 40-42	New records of Lepidoptera from Nepal (listing 37 species)
2011	Bionotes, ALIGARH No.13 p.63- 69	(Some) Butterflies of Pokhara Valley, Nepal (251 species listed)
2012	Bionotes, ALIGARH No.14 p.50, 51	Abundance of Butterflies on *Poinsettia* tree. (50 species a listed)

(B) Articles in Popular Magazines

1988	Nepal Traveler 5(10) p.17	Butterflies of Nepal
1989	Prakriti 2(2)	Are Nepal's Butterflies in Danger?
1990	Nepal Traveler 7(4) p.39	A Butterfly Walk in Pokhara Valley
1991	Shangri-La 2(3)	Flying Colours
1995	Welcome Nepal 3(2) p.41	Nepal's Butterflies – Winter & Spring
1996	Welcome Nepal 4(1) p.26	Peculiarities of Butterfly Behaviour

| 1997 | To-Day 15(2) p.23 | Nepal - A Butterfly's Paradise |

(C) Books

1989 & 1994	Craftsman Press Bangkok (350p.)	BUTTERFLIES of NEPAL (listing 643 species)
1993 & 2006	Craftsman Bangkok, Bangkok 28p.	ILLUSTRATED CHECKLIST of NEPAL'S BUTTERFLIES (653species)
1995	Know Nepal Series No.14 (80p.)	BUTTERFLIES of ROYAL CHITWAN NAT. PARK (247 species)
1998	Know Nepal Series No.13 (112p.)	BUTTERFLIES of KATHMANDU VALLEY (359 sp.)
2010	Himalayan Nature 184p. 10 pl.	LEPIDOPTERA of NEPAL - checklist (660 Butts + 3,900 Moths)
2011	Himalayan Map house 144p.	POCKET BOOK OF BUTTERFLIES OF NEPAL in Natural Environment (278 species all illustrated
2011	ACAP (Sigma Press) 154 p.	BUTTERFLIES OF THE ANNAPURNA CONSERVATION AREA (347 species)

2017	Libird (provided information) 174 sp.	Butterflies of Begnas Watershed

(D) Booklets

1990	Know Nepal Series no.3 (32p.)	Beautiful Butterflies (266 sp. illustrated)
2003 & 2007	Kathmandu University (60p.)	Lepidopterous Insects described from Nepal - (Black & White) (940 taxa)
2007 & 2011	NMA (for Int. Mount Mus) (16p. 44 figs.)	20 Butterfly Questions & Answers (particularly relating to Nepal)
2013	Himalayan Maphouse12p (60 figs)	Butterflies of Nepal - month by month = (Calendar for 2013)
2018 (copy frp, 2007 K.U.)	24p. 8 plates	DIURNAL Lepidopterous Insects (Checklist)

www.ingramcontent.com/pod-product-compliance
Lightning Source LLC
Chambersburg PA
CBHW050030090426
42735CB00021B/3437